NATURE'S TRANQUILITY

REFLECTIONS AND INSIGHTS

INTRODUCTION BY
TOM KLEIN

NorthWord Press
Minnetonka, Minnesota

What is Nature?

It is an eagle soaring over spruce spires; a canoe gliding silently over cold, clear waters; a wolf pack slipping stealthily through the timber; the haunting wail of a loon echoing across the shrouded ripples of a secluded lake. It is the jagged granite outcrops and gnarled, windswept trees of a sprawling, rugged wilderness.

Nature is all of that and so much more. Nature is a spiritual home. It has quiet power. It works slowly and relentlessly on your psyche. It gets into your blood, into your *soul*.

Within these pages you will find evocative descriptions and ponderings by some very insightful naturalists. Their perceptions and remembrances, along with stunning photography, bring to us all a tiny reflection of Nature's incomparable diversity, so that we may always cherish the spirit of Nature's Tranquility.

— TOM KLEIN

My father, you have spoken well;
you have told me that heaven is very
beautiful; tell me now one thing more.
Is it more beautiful than the country of
the musk ox in summer, when sometimes
the mist blows over the lakes, and
sometimes the water is blue, and the
 loons cry very often?

– Saltatha, a Yellowknife Indian

A lake is the landscape's most beautiful and expressive feature. It is earth's eye; looking into which the beholder measures the depth of his own nature. The fluviatile trees next the shore are the slender eyelashes which fringe it, and the wooded hills and cliffs around are its overhanging brows.

– Henry David Thoreau

Where Leopold once saw the fierce green fire in the dying wolf's eyes we can look into the eyes of the black bear more closely and see it – alive. What we see is almost incomprehensible. But not quite. We are, after all, just beginning to learn about our world again, the second time around. Poised between a past we cannot afford to lose and a mountain of impending truth, we find ourselves in another type of Kawishiwi country – this no place between – by a rapid river flowing across the broad and factual continent of our intelligence. Searching for our bearings. Circling overhead, in a stellar performance mocking our own lives, the great skybear stalks her infinite territory, followed forever by a single cub who carries true North in the tip of his tail.

— Jeff Fair

Only to the white man was nature a wilderness
and only to him was the land 'infested' with 'wild'
animals and 'savage' people. To us it was tame.
Earth was bountiful and we were surrounded with
the blessings of the Great Mystery.

> – Chief Luther Standing Bear
> of the Oglala Sioux

North is a state of mind,
not a geographic delineation.

> – Tom Klein

But can't you hear the wild?
It's calling you.
Let us probe the silent places,
Let us seek what luck betide us;
Let us journey to a lonely land I know.
There's a whisper on the night wind,
There's a star agleam to guide us,
And the Wind is calling . . .
Let us go.

– Robert Service

The North keeps getting
further north every year.

– Anonymous

Above all, it is wild nature itself in this region that charms. To be able to follow unfamiliar watercourses days, weeks and months, to contend with wind and wave, to sleep in the open under pines or beside leaping water, to view sun and shadow on the changing scene of woodland, rock, and water, to hobnob with the wild creatures of the north, in short to lose oneself in the profusion of original America – all this is the cherished dream of every true American.

– Ernest C. Oberholtzer

Once in his life a man ought to concentrate his mind upon the remembered earth. He ought to give himself up to a particular landscape in his experience; to look at it from as many angles as he can, to wonder upon it, to dwell upon it. He ought to imagine that he touches it with his hands at every season and listens to the sounds that are made upon it. He ought to imagine the creatures there and all the faintest motions of the wind. He ought to recollect the glare of the moon and the colors of the dawn and dusk.

– N. Scott Momaday

For the animal shall not be measured by man. In a world older and more complete than ours they move finished and complete, gifted with extensions of the senses we have lost or never attained, living by voices we shall never hear. They are not brethren, they are not underlings; they are other nations, caught with ourselves in the net of life and time, fellow prisoners of the splendor and travail of the earth.

— Henry Beston

Is not the sky a father and the earth
a mother and are not all living things with feet
or wing or roots their children?

– Black Elk

I have seen maybe a thousand northern lakes,
and they all look alike in many ways, but there was
something different about that little lake that held
me hard. I sat there perhaps half an hour,
like a man under a spell, just looking it over.

– John J. Rowlands

There's gold, and it's haunting
and haunting;
It's luring me on as of old;
Yet it isn't the gold that I'm wanting
So much as just finding the gold.
It's the great, big, broad land
'way up yonder,
It's the forests where silence has lease;
It's the beauty that thrills me with wonder,
It's the stillness that fills me with peace.

– Robert Service

I am glad I shall never be young
without wild country to be young
in. What avail are forty freedoms without a
blank spot on the map?

— Aldo Leopold

It's very sad if our culture only
sees wilderness as a place to
play. What wilderness should be doing is
speaking to our souls and teaching us about
being quiet...and respecting the world we
live in.

— Bill Mason

To anyone who has spent a winter in the
north and known the depths to which the
snow can reach, known the weeks when the
mercury stays below zero, the first hint of
spring is a major event. You must live in the
north to understand it. You cannot
just come up for it as you might
go to Florida for the sunshine
and the surf. To appreciate it, you must
go through considerable enduring.

— Sigurd F. Olson

The Lord did well when he put the loon and his music into this lonesome land.

– Aldo Leopold

Something lost behind the ranges,
Something hidden, go and find it.
Go and look behind the ranges,
Something lost behind the ranges,
Lost and waiting for you. Go.

– Rudyard Kipling

This is a delicious evening, when the whole body is one sense, and imbibes delight through every pore. I go and come with a strange liberty in Nature, a part of herself. As I walk along the stony shore of the pond in my shirt sleeves, though it is cool as well as cloudy and windy, and I see nothing special to attract me, all the elements are unusually congenial to me. The bull frogs trump to usher in the night, and the note of the whip-poorwill is borne on the rippling wind from over the water. Sympathy with the fluttering alder and poplar leaves almost takes away my breath; yet, like the lake, my serenity is rippled but not ruffled.

– Henry David Thoreau

While one can argue about where the north precisely begins, we instinctively know when we've arrived. In the North the ribbons of highways to the south are replaced by winding rivers. Instead of the neon and amber lights of downstate cities are stars in the heavens above so bright that they seem nearer to the earth. The howl of the wolf or call of the coyote is more likely to be heard than the siren of a police car or the thunder of a jet. A defining difference, quite simply, is that in the northwoods there are more white-tailed deer than Fords, more lakes than shopping malls.

– Mark Peterson

The northwoods is one of the most recently uncovered places in the world. Less than 10,000 years ago, while civilization was well underway in the Middle East, parts of the northwoods were still under an ice cap that stood two miles high in places. The enormous weight of the ice caused the lower layer to bulge outward in all directions, bulldozing mountains and gouging the earth as it moved. Frigid air swooped down from the front of the glacier, creating a wide fringe of tundra wherever it went. When the glacier finally stopped and began to melt backwards, great muddy torrents roared over its cliffs and rushed out through tunnels in its face. Their payload of crushed rock, gravel, sand and ice settled over hundreds of miles to form the lake-splattered landscape that we know today.

– Janine Benyus

We once knew the wolf. We behaved as it did. We tried to capture some of its spirit, to learn from it how to hunt, and the social rules of the hunting group. We must have learned well, for we are still here, thriving, after a fashion, and we have no more need for the teacher.

— Denny Olson

I have always been impressed by the scale and grandeur of the canoe country. It is a hard and boney land and, were it not for the linking waterways of the area, would scarcely be penetrable. Unlike the grand vistas of mountain country, the canoe country allows you only glimpses of its magnitude. Almost furtively it leads you on, down narrow lakes or winding rivers, opening itself only gradually to the explorer. One can sit atop a mountain and contemplate an entire region; in the canoe country one sits only on small lichen-covered knobs, surveying intimate scenes. But it is exactly this shyness that is the canoe country's charm and one must probe it slowly and over long years before knowing many of its secrets, before sensing its grandeur.

— Michael Furtman

Ecosystems are like intimate human relationships; the components need and nourish each other while demanding independence and space; changes in one bring about changes in the other, there are phases and cycles, the changes tuned to time; and there are constants represented by the life processes that make it possible for the systems to flourish in different forms when trauma disrupts or removes a component. Just as human relationships mature over years, so do ecosystem communities over a longer period. A big tree forest, for example, comes into being over several centuries.

– Robert Trever

In our everyday world of human-made, human-scale things, we are inclined to think rather well of ourselves. We are *Homo sapiens*, after all, and even in this day of evolutionary enlightenment generally view ourselves as favored offspring of the universe. It takes an eagle to bring us down to size. Though only a fraction of our weight, these birds dwarf us; for by soaring into the sky, they give a tangible, vertical dimension to the observable world. They offer us a measure of the heavens and, as they disappear above the clouds, hint at spheres beyond our sphere to which we have no ready access. Perhaps we are not the center of things after all, not so very large, not so powerful. With all the finesse of modern technology, we can't ride the air like the eagles. We can't even come close.

– Candace Savage

The singing wilderness has to do with the calling of
the loons, northern lights, and the great silences
of a land lying north of Lake Superior. It is con-
cerned with the simple joys, the timelessness and the
perspective found in a way of life that is close to the
past. I have discovered that I am not
alone in my listening; that almost every-
one is listening for something, that the
search for places where the singing may
be heard goes on everywhere. It seems to
be part of the hunger that all of us have for a time
when we were closer to lakes and rivers, to mountains
and meadows and forests, than we are today . . .
We may not know exactly what it is we are listening
for, but we hunt as instinctively for opportunities and
places to listen as sick animals look for healing herbs.

– Sigurd F. Olson

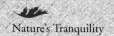

I rejoice that there are owls. Let them do the idiotic and maniacal hooting for men. It is a sound admirably suited to swamps and twilight woods which no day illustrates, suggesting a vast and undeveloped nature which men have not recognized. They represent the stark twilight and unsatisfied thoughts which we all have.

– Henry David Thoreau

No one can weigh or measure culture, hence I shall waste no time trying to do so. Suffice it to say that by common consent of thinking people, there are cultural values in the sports, customs and experiences that renew contacts with wild things.

– Aldo Leopold

Our tent is on the northern tip of the island. We look out past a great sweep of pine bough to the waters of our lake and the silent misty one beyond. **This is the moment**, I think, when I've really given my heart to our canoe country, though I've been entranced with it from the first. But here its special quality of wild innocence touches me sharply and deeply.

– Florence Page Jaques

The North Country is a siren. Who can resist her song of intricate and rich counterpoint – the soaring harmonies of bird melodies against an accompaniment of lapping waters, roaring cataracts, and the soft, sad overtones of pine boughs? Her flowing garments are forever green, the rich velvet verdure of pine needles. In autumn she pricks out the green background with embroidery of gold here and scarlet there. Winter adds a regal touch, with gleaming diamonds in her hair and ermine billowing from her shoulders. Those who have ever seen her in her beauty or listened to her vibrant melodies can never quite forget her nor lose the urge to return to her.

– Grace Lee Nute

Years ago, a friend who lived on the seashore was shocked to learn that the admired scent of salt air was due in part to the odor of decomposing marine organisms. But knowing this should not detract from anyone's fun at the beach, where, after all, the sun still shines as brightly, and the waves still break into foam. Nor should it detract from our enjoyment of the woods to know that brilliant fall colors foretell the imminent wholesale death of once-green leaves preparing to go to earth and decay. It might even heighten our enjoyment of autumn, by lending a sense of urgency to the task of getting out into the country before the colors fade and the trees drop their foliage. In recent years more people than ever have apparently felt this urgency, because autumn foliage has been attracting tourists and travelers by the millions to wooded areas. Each fall the inns are filled, buses are chartered, cars crowd the highways, and bikers and hikers hit the roads and trails as legions of leaf-peepers open their eyes to nature's extravagance. And extravagance it seems to be, for there appears to be no good reason for a tree to take on scarlet, gold or wine. A brilliant flower can attract the pollinating insect or bird it needs for the plant's reproduction, but a brilliant leaf attracts only the gaze of its admirer.

— Ron Lanner

It is snowing today. The scent of the snow is manifest. The spruce are powdered deep, the soft plumes of the great white pines are overlaid with films of silver. White flakes tumble thick and fast, brushing against my face like evanescent butterflies. All the peace that this country has given us comes showering down around us in the heavy snowfall. Our departure, in this mood, is beautiful to me. Without a pang I see the myriad footprints, which we have made along our shore and in the ice-held forest, vanish beneath the drifting snowflakes.

– Florence Page Jaques

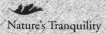
It is something to be alone in the bush,
the wind in the trees and the feeling that if there are
such things as big cities, they must have existed in
some ancient past. It is a fine thing to climb a rise, sit
in the weeds, smoke a pipe and look off for miles at
more of the same country you just came through.

– Gordon MacQuarrie

On this winter night, the wilderness waits —
a reservoir of silence and darkness held for
safekeeping in a world of noise and street-
lights. It is a gift to the few who live along its
edge, and to many who do not. Perhaps
most importantly, it is a gift held in
trust for those whose lives have
not yet begun. The wolves are its night
watchmen, the stars its only lamps.

— David Olesen

The way of the canoe is the way of the wilderness and of a freedom almost forgotten. It is an antidote to insecurity, the open door to waterways of ages past and a way of life with profound and abiding satisfactions. When a man is part of his canoe, he is part of all that canoes have ever known.

– Sigurd F. Olson

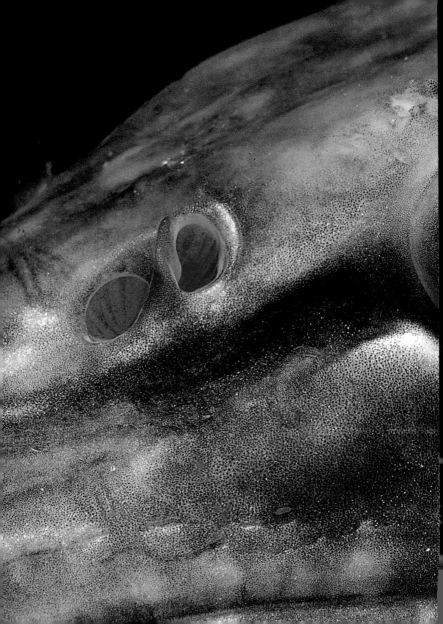

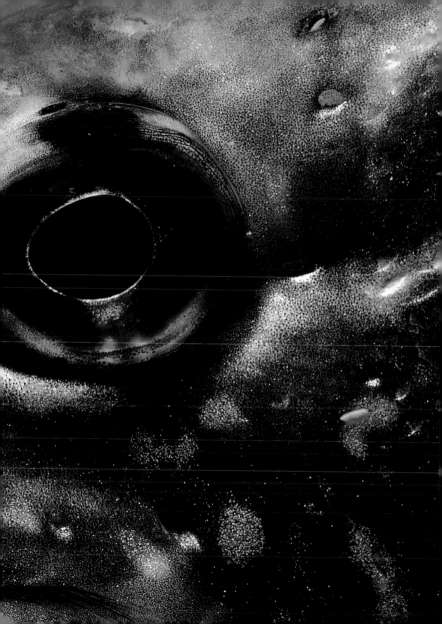

Many people clearly recall their first experience with loons, and people almost always remember the first time they heard loon music. I'm slightly embarrassed to admit I don't. While boyhood trips to northern Wisconsin produced a few loon encounters, nothing special happened. It wasn't until August of 1965 on the Minnesota-Canada border that loons grabbed my soul. With Bill Richtsmeier, a high school buddy, I drove to Moose Lake, a little ways north of Ely, to start a great Boundary Waters adventure. After a long day's paddle and portage, we made it to Louisa Falls at the bottom of Agnes Lake, just over the Canadian border. Shoulders bright red from the August sun and sore from the sharp bite of the

thin Duluth pack straps, we settled into the
campsite surrounded by a reassuring audio back-
drop of falling water. The loons on Agnes called
that night, probably no louder nor more often than
they do on any other August night. But the calling
found the right spot. We sat by the campfire
bewitched, anticipating two weeks of granite cliffs,
water diamonds on the shimmering lakes, firm lake
trout, spongy sphagnum moss and quiet evenings
with the voices of the wilderness. That night on
Agnes we didn't know the difference between the
tremolo, wail or yodel. And we didn't care.
We just soaked it all in. It was a magical
night. I haven't kept track of Bill over the passing
years so I can't speak for him, but nothing has
been the same for me since.

— Tom Klein

Appears to have been much frequented by the savages of old, as may be judged from the various figures of animals & c. made by them on the face of the steep Rock. Amongst them may be seen fish, flesh, and Tortoise all of them painted with some kind of Red Paint. These figures are made by scratching the Rock weed (moss) off the Rocks with the Point of a knife or some other instrument.

– John Macdonell

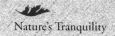

We need to preserve a few places, a few
samples of primeval country so that when the pace gets
too fast we can look at it, think about it, contemplate it,
and somehow restore equanimity to our souls.

— Sigurd F. Olson

And the evening sun descending
Set the clouds on fire with redness,
Burned the broad sky like a prairie
Left upon the level water
One long track and trail of splendor
Down whose stream, as down a river,
Westward, westward Hiawatha
Sailed into the fiery sunset
Sailed into the purple vapors
Sailed into the dusk of evening.

— Longfellow